WEEKLY WR READER®
EARLY LEARNING LIBRARY

Let's Read About

Weather

Let's Read About

Sun

by Susan Nations

**Reading Consultant: Susan Nations, M.Ed.,
author/literacy coach/consultant
in literacy development**

Please visit our web site at: www.garethstevens.com
For a free color catalog describing Weekly Reader® Early Learning Library's list of high-quality books, call 1-877-445-5824 (USA) or 1-800-387-3178 (Canada). Weekly Reader® Early Learning Library's fax: (414) 336-0164.

Library of Congress Cataloging-in-Publication Data

Nations, Susan.
    Let's read about sun / by Susan Nations.
        p. cm. — (Let's read about weather)
    ISBN-13: 978-0-8368-7807-3 (lib. bdg.)
    ISBN-13: 978-0-8368-7812-7 (softcover)
    1. Sun—Juvenile literature.   I. Title.
QB521.5.N38   2006
523.7—dc22   2006029351

This edition first published in 2007 by
Weekly Reader® Early Learning Library
A Member of the WRC Media Family of Companies
330 West Olive Street, Suite 100
Milwaukee, WI 53212 USA

Editor: Dorothy L. Gibbs
Art direction: Tammy West
Cover design and page layout: Dave Kowalski
Photo research: Diane Laska-Swanke

Picture credits: Cover, title, © Richard Hutchings/PhotoEdit; p. 4 U.S. Fish and Wildlife Service; pp. 5, 12 (upper left) © Cleo Photography/PhotoEdit; p. 6 © David Young-Wolff/PhotoEdit; pp. 7, 12 (upper right) © Robert W. Ginn/PhotoEdit; p. 8 © David Frazier/PhotoEdit; p. 9 NOAA; p. 10 © Jeff Greenberg/PhotoEdit; p. 11 © Felicia Martinez/PhotoEdit; p. 12 (lower left and right) © Diane Laska-Swanke

Printed in the United States of America

1 2 3 4 5 6 7 8 9 10 10 09 08 07 06

Note to Educators and Parents

Learning to read is one of the most exciting and challenging things young children do. Among other skills, they are beginning to match the spoken word to print and learn directionality and print conventions. Books that are appropriate for emergent readers will incorporate many of these conventions while also being appealing and entertaining.

The books in the *Let's Read About Weather* series are designed to support young readers in the earliest stages of literacy. They will love looking at the full-color photographs while learning about the exciting variety of weather. Each book will invite children to read — and reread — again and again!

In addition to serving as wonderful picture books in schools, libraries, and homes, this series is specifically intended to be read within instructional small groups. The small group setting enables the teacher or other adult to provide scaffolding that will boost the reader's efforts. Children and adults alike will find these books supportive, engaging, and fun!

— Susan Nations, M.Ed., author/literacy coach/
consultant in literacy development

Sun on the bird.

Sun on the boat.

Sun on the towel.

Sun on the float.

Sun on the sand.

Sun on the sea.

Sun on the shovel.

Sun on me!

Glossary

boat

float

shovel

towel